Who am I?

A selection of reflective poems

Fatema Valji

In the Name of God, The Kind, The Merciful

Published by Sun Behind The Cloud Publications Ltd
PO Box 15889, Birmingham, B16 6NZ

This edition first published in 2019
© Copyright Fatema Valji

All rights reserved.
No part of this publication may be reproduced by any means
without the express permission of the publisher.

ISBN (print): 978-1-908110-54-1
ISBN (ebook): 978-1-908110-55-8

A CIP catalogue record of this book is available
from the British Library.

www.sunbehindthecloud.com
info@sunbehindthecloud.com

There is a candle in your heart,
ready to be kindled.
There is a void in your soul,
ready to be filled.
You feel it, don't you?

Rumi

Contents

Preface	6
Who am I?	8
Reality	10
Seeking through a Void	12
Night	14
Disconnected	15
Bubbles	16
Loneliness	18
Solitude	20
Chameleon	22
Lure of the Sea	24
Beauty	26
The Sea	28
Between Worlds	31
Awakening	34
Nature	36
Blindness	38
Dirty Dishes	40
Teacher	43
Mother	46

My Shadow	48
Empathy	50
A Mother in Palestine	52
Silent Plea	54
Liberty	56
Born to Dream	58
Compassion	60
Plastic	62
Façades	64
Irony	66
How Conscious am I?	69
Runaway Train	70
To what End	72
Time	74
Whirlwhind	76
Maybe Later	78
Vision	80
Freedom	82

Preface

'There is a widespread sense of loss here, if not always of God, then at least of meaning.'[1] (Charles Taylor, *A Secular Age*)

We live in a highly sensory, digitised world, saturated with all the advantages of scientific and material advancement. Naturally, we live healthier, longer and more comfortable lives than ever before.

Our overflowing cup, however, is not without a drop of bitterness. Sometimes, our lives spiral into circular discontent. In the unrelenting pursuit of materialistic objectives, we may be left with a gnawing sense of loss deep within.

A malaise of meaninglessness - 'depthlessness'[2] - seems to afflict our societies. Yet, as we manage rising levels of depression, alcoholism, addiction and tedium with drugs and distraction, do we consider that maybe, an inner void might also spawn our disquiet?

The contemporary philosopher, Charles Taylor, suggests that whilst modern man may be alienated from spirituality, he still yearns for a 'sense of fullness… of peace or wholeness; or able to act on that level, of integrity or generosity or abandonment or self-forgetfulness.'[3]

---

1. Taylor, Charles. *A Secular Age*, Harvard University Press, 2009, p.552.

2. Jameson, Fredric. *Postmodernism, Or, The Cultural Logic of Late Capitalism*, Durham, Duke University Press, 1991.

3. Taylor, C. *A Secular Age*, Harvard University Press, 2009, p. 5.

Indeed, we are more than bodies that desire and machines that function. Our souls' joy and fulfilment lie in transcendence. We long to see, feel and breathe more deeply; to free ourselves from worldly obsessions so we can rise higher, be better.

Poetry is one set of wings that enables us to soar. It allows us to move beyond the realm of matter to one of meaning, so that we can interiorise and actualise immaterial truths and ideals.

This collection of poems is not a biographical or personal account. Rather, I have assumed a voice that reflects a generic quest for purpose and growth within and beyond ordinary, day to day aspects and relationships of life. The poems express an inner conversation that I hope, resonates in the relatability of the dilemmas, aspirations, hopes and fears explored. They probe our quintessentially human longing to reach the deeper truth and objectives of this journey of endless possibility that we call life.

I invite you to turn the page and join me in seeking beauty, purpose and the subtle 'something more' that makes life meaningful.

Fatema Valji
February 2019

Who am I?

I am mud,
The quintessence of dust,
Humble grit, non-descript

Yet within my grime lies
A ray of His pure light,
Colourless, raceless, non-finite

In spirit, I am unbound
By cliques, prejudice,
Power, hierarchies

Unhardened and undefined,
Soft and pure, love and light,
Mercy, grace, truth personified

Earthly body, spirit divine,
Transcending pettiness, selfishness,
With compassion, liberal heart and mind

Until I descend into pretense,
Rigidities, contempt of difference,
Sham pride, divides, defines,
Oh what a fool am I!

Consumed by spite and exclusivity,
Detaching and defaming, hating and blaming,
Snuffing my humanity, soiling my dignity,
Muck and filth personified

Dirt or divine, the choice is mine,
Ignore the agony, injustice,
A spiritless, clay marionette
Or with iron will, act, reject!

Am I the flicker of active, burning love
As the darkness spreads?
Or merely cold cynicism, passive at best?
Caring only for myself and mine
While communities shatter, ignorance reigns,

Deaf, dumb, blind
I am light extinguished,
Dead earth, buried alive

Reality

What a strange world we live in!

Where truth is only veritable,
If it's measurable, observable,
Literal

If you can see it
Or substantiate it
With data empirical,
Then it's reality
Is unequivocal

Everything else
Is like unicorns and elves,
Fanciful, mythical,
Unreal

A bright rose amongst weeds
Is merely the growth of a seed,
A soaring crow
Rarely uplifts the soul,

A caterpillar transforms into a butterfly
And I hardly bat an eye

It's a natural cycle
Rather than a wondrous miracle,
Or a beautiful, spiritual metaphor

Beauty, meaning, poetry,
All that transcends, eludes me
Because reality is corporeal,
Prosaic and two-dimensional

What a pity,
I do not see
How material details
Shadow and veil
The essence of reality

Seeking Through a Void

When smouldering tears ran dry,
Yet the anguish would not subside
When sorrow scavenged all peace,
Leaving my heart gaunt with grief,
I realised

When I saw my dreams, my goals,
One by one, disintegrate, dissolve
When I thought my insides would explode,
A volcano of shattered hopes,
I realised

When I was with people but utterly forlorn,
Smiling, composed, as loneliness gnawed my soul
When I struggled to find the eye of serenity
In the storm of my soul's duplicity,
I realised

When I was inflamed by anger and pain,
Suffering injustice, paying for others' mistakes
When I struggled to forbear, forgive, forget,
Keep my resentment in check,
I realised

When death claimed a friend
And sorrow overwhelmed
When loss deprived me of sleep,
Focus, energy, peace,
I realised

I realised what in ease, I never perceived
How needy I was, vulnerable, utterly weak!
How arrogant, foolish, to think I could manage myself,
Suffice as my own master, compass and friend!

No wonder I was haunted by fear, broken by pain,
Consumed by anger, drowning in despair
I tried to go it alone - alone I was bound to fail

I realised all strength and solace flow from one Source
So why seek peace in desire's futile course?

If I truly empty and open my heart, only for Him,
All strength, peace, and joy will surely flood in

Night

A mantle of darkness
Covers my conspicuousness

Finally,

In welcome seclusion,
I am free to shed all illusions

Finally,

I can cast aside
Guile and guise
I can retreat within,
Examine
My estranged spirit

Finally,

I can face
The secrets buried deep inside,
Void behind my plastic smile,
Sorrows crying to be healed,
My listless soul's longing for peace

Perhaps, it's time,
I was acquainted
With my true self

Disconnected

Behind the wheel,
Revving, accelerating, steering steel,
Doors barred, windows sealed
Nature's rhythm, beauty - remote, concealed,
Automated reflexes, door-to-door routine
Merging as one, self and machine

Fully-equipped, high-tech home,
Gadget-cluttered, gadget-controlled,
Over-stocked with amenities, comforts,
Diversions, sensory overload,
Minimising any inclination to venture outdoors

So I slouch, sedentary,
Eyes glazed, glued
To smart-phone, tablet, kindle, tube
Barely breathing, vegetating, hibernating,
Tapping, clicking, endlessly uploading, updating,
Vacant heart, numb soul,
Uninspired, pallid, cold

Isolated from nature's poetry,
Vigour and vitality,
Desensitised,
Dehumanised,
I am a lemming of modernity

Bubbles

When I was younger,
I would gaze with wonder

As the bubbles I blew
Caught the light,
Glinting,
Glistening,
Softly reflecting
A myriad of rainbows bright

I marvelled
At their delicacy,
Perfect symmetry,
How they floated in the breeze,
Danced as they pleased,
Graceful,
Exquisite,
Free

Until
They vanished,
Disappeared into the wind,
Leaving no trace
Of beauty or grace

Years later,
I wonder…

Am I still misled
By gleaming emptiness,
A child beguiled
By spurious success?

Loneliness

In a crowd, but on my own,
Surrounded, yet alone,
Socialising, wiling time,
With a pasted, hollow smile

What I really think,
I keep within
What I see and feel,
I don't reveal

Not because I'm not free
To lift my mask of bland conformity,
It's just that I'm afraid
My thoughts won't resonate
With the lilting chatter.

And I'd rather not interrupt,
Only to be dubbed
A spoiler of fun,
Boring stick in the mud

And yet,

All the floating and flitting
Leaves my mind spinning

I follow the shifts -
From holiday planning, weight-loss techniques, to gossip,
Work routines, new restaurants, to fashion tips,
Feeling slightly sick...

To what end?

Where are these frothy conversations going?
In all the verbal to-ing and fro-ing,
Where is the quest for meaning,
Divine purpose and being?

Perhaps you've been there too,
Torn between melting in the stew
And changing the essential flavour,
Risking censure

And maybe, like me,
You always give in
To the desire to fit in

If only...

We could forego our obsession
With self-preservation
And show a little more courage
To lead the conversation

It might make all the difference.

Solitude

I'm
Caught,
Entangled,
Besieged

By an ensnaring,
Constraining,
Suffocating,
Social web

I chafe
Against the strain
Of laboured conversation,
Pressured expectation,
Contrived integration,

My spirit smothered, squeezed,
Struggling to breathe

So I retreat
Into an inner world,
Uncontrolled
By others

Where I am free
To interact and be
With my own ideas, emotions,
Ideals, values, vision,

Undisturbed,
Uncurbed,
Uncensured...

My gratitude overflows,
How well He knows!

My need to reclaim
Self and faith
Through solitude's
Saving grace.

Chameleon

Have I considered the chameleon?

Sometimes a fresh, incandescent green
Blending into sun-dappled leaves,
Sometimes a murky, dull brown
Half-buried in the forest ground

Of what relevance is this mere lizard to my life?
Its ways are bestial; I'm human and far more civilised!
A chameleon is a creature of instinct: no mind and soul
I have a spirit that aspires and grows

And yet, is not the chameleon's genius for deception
Almost human in conception?
Its power to adapt and blend in
Akin to my assimilating to fit in?

Are we so different, the chameleon and I?
Yes, I may be mammal, she a reptile
But a deeper look reveals
We are twins of duplicity and deceit

As I connive my way in society,
Have I more courage than a lizard, more integrity?

Doesn't even the chameleon's camouflage pale
Before my changing colours, varying shades?

In a world of materialism and vanity,
I have managed to fit in perfectly
I've sold my soul and identity
For a cheap veneer of superficiality

By nature, the chameleon is shifty in shade and hue
Yet I am human! My essence reproaches me to be true
'Break free of conformity and artifice,' it cries

I hang my head, whisper my cowardly reply,
'But it's so much easier living a lizard's lie!'

Lure of the Sea

What is it about the sea
That makes the eyes dreamy,
Heart tranquil,
Soul breathe easy?

Is the lure of the ocean
In her glimmering inflection
Or silent stillness?

Is the beauty of the sea
In her grace and poetry,
Depth and subtlety,

Or does her charm rest
In her soothing caress,
Light rhythm and perfumed cadences,
Gratifying all my senses?

Does the sea evoke laughter,
Abandon and playful rapture,
Her flow and sparkle enticing me to a quest
For endless rest and amusement?

Or do I gaze past ocean froth and fore
To a deeper world beyond the shore,

Do I forego lazing at the beach
To seek the Source of love and peace?

In the sea, do I see
Clarity, transparency,
An infinite mirror of light and beauty,
Love and Majesty,

Or am I more entranced
By the waves' merry dance,
Inviting me to surf and snorkel on the surface,
Soak in the joy of the moment?

Perhaps the sea's call
Echoes the longing of my own soul,
If it's sun-soaked frolic I seek,
So I receive

And if I seek vision
Beyond illusion,
Then the journey to Infinity, Peace,
The sea reveals

Beauty

In considering the world's complexity,
Intricate design and diversity,
I deduce with wonder:
How logically necessary is the Originator,
Grand Creator!

Definitely,
Perfect design
Is evident proof
Of intelligence divine,

Yet I prefer to suspend my logical mind
And open an eye more subtle, sublime
To seek, to savour,
Not fact or reason,
But beauty divine

More compelling, more revealing
Than all rational reasoning
Is the luminous splendour around me,
Disclosing, manifesting, glorifying
Divinity

Delicate, dewy tulips in bloom,
Scarlet rose-buds flowering in June,

Tall pines gracing majestic peaks,
Bejewelling lush, green, valleys,

Still and starry nights,
Powdery snow bathed in light,
Birches, maples, sycamores
Shedding leaves in ruddy glows

I drink in the beauty, let it seep
Into my soul, deep
I do not analyse, I do not critique,
I merely see, feel
And weep

The Sea

At the edge of the sea,
I stand,
Still

Awed
By her luminescence,
Azure translucence,
A blue infused,
Consumed,
Subsumed
By the Immanent!

I gaze
Into infinity,
Seamless perennity,
No beginning, no end,
Passing time, fading sequence,
Only eternal, abiding
Presence

I sense
A depth and breadth
Of Love so immense,
I know,
No parched soul drenched,

Remains unquenched

And so, I'm drawn
By Love's irresistible tide,
Gently pulling me nigh,
Beauty and grace divine
Tugging at my knotted inside

How I yearn
To spurn
My dark, shadowy plight,
Dive into the light!

And yet,
I pause.

Between distraction and devotion,
Caprice and conviction,
Earth and Heaven,
I'm torn

Am I willing to commit
Every fibre of my spirit
To truth and virtue alone?
Will I abandon
Desires wanton
And transcend
My selfish self?

Only then,
Can I be
A drop in the sea,
At one
With Love,
Beauty,
He

Between worlds

Yesterday, whilst walking to school,
My daughter said,

*'But why do we have to use newspaper instead
Of wrapping paper like everyone else?'*

'To save our beautiful trees,' I replied
'But trees are plentiful', she sighed

*'Look over there… and there… and there,
Trees are everywhere!'*

'Yes,' I smiled
*'But I wish you could see
The difference between sparse, urban trees
And towering giants
Thickly cloaking forests
In majesty.'*

I wonder if,

Growing up in a disposable, plastic age,
She can ever really understand or appreciate,
The profundity, beauty,
Essentiality,
Of an ancient tree

A tree that lifts your gaze so high,
You feel your soul touch the sky,
A tree that has breathed
Divine glory and mercy
For centuries

My child has never embraced
An ancient tree with friends,
Four pairs of arms that extend
Round a trunk so immense, rooted and tall,
They catch their breath in awe

She has never sat quietly
On wet moss 'neath a forest canopy
Inhaling fresh, woody incense,
In deep, dewy, stillness

Or stood on an alpine ridge
Above pines piercing the mist,
Pristine, sheer,
Ethereal

Only to turn to her right,
To find
Decimation,
Black and utter desolation
Forests burnt, clear-cut,
All life reduced
To barren dust

And so,
I worry...

Will she ever see,
How her choices daily,
Impact
This dark dichotomy?

Awakening

Darkness fades,
Dimmed by glowing shades,
Azure tinged with lilac hues,
Light and fire radiating the blues

Dawn's soft blush
Deepens into a crimson flush
Kissed by light's gold,
Morn's reticent rose
Bursts into resplendent marigold

Effusion of colour and light,
Exuding awe, delight,
Glorifying divine grace
In silent hymns of reverent praise

Amidst lilting melody,
Ode to perfect divinity
Birds in song, wings in flight,
Aspiring towards His pleasure,
Soaring towards His light

Below, the oak is still,
Affixed by His glory and will

As He bids and beckons,
Its branches bend, leaves descend

Nature awakens every morn
To diffuse His light at dawn,
Yet how many dawns pass and fade
Whilst I slumber away,
Unroused by her recurring call:

'Awaken! Arise!
Actualise divine beauty and light!'

Nature

Once, we loved her,
Cherished her as a selfless mother
Humbled by her grace,
We sought divine mercy in her embrace

We revered the scent of her hair
At her feet, we rushed to prayer
In her lap, we grew wise
In her beauty, we found the Divine

She was beauty and light manifest
In honouring her, our souls were blessed
In preserving her,
We fulfilled the divine order

Only when we forsook our station
As His slave and agent,
Allowing material desire
To snuff our light and fire,

Did we become nature's conquerors,
Promethian industrialisers
Our sole motivation, intent,
To secure a worldly end

We manipulated, destroyed,
Forests, seas, soil,
For concrete, smog and plastic,
Opulence, power and profit

Now we only have a small window of time,
Before we lose the little that survives
Our only hope is to reclaim, revive,
The divine role we cast aside

No green campaign can truly succeed,
Until we humbly accede,
We are not masters of the universe,
We are her humble agents

Let us awaken to responsibility,
Before He looks us in the eye, squarely,
Asking plainly,
'*O humanity, how did you fulfil your sacred trust,*
To serve and conserve this beautiful earth?'

Blindness

I live in a world of wisdom and design,
Breath and brush-stroke divine,
Where every raindrop, falling leaf,
From His Hand is released

Yet still I moan about rainy days,
Inconvenience, mud and grey,
Downpours may be floods of grace,
But all I perceive, is traffic and delays

Head down, I rush around,
Always on the move, never in the now
No pause,
To catch His smile through the clouds,
Or tune in to the wind
To hear Him whisper aloud

Material obsessions delude my heart and mind
The world is a career highway, a gold mine,
To be exploited and stripped bare,
Rather than divine unveiling, inspiring awe and prayer

And so,
I do not see His reflection in morning dew,
The depths of divine mercy in oceans blue

My heart is unstirred by the tide's ebb and flow,
Unlit by the splendour of sunset's glow

Nature discloses the Beloved's face
But my heart averts its gaze
His love resonates in her song and silence
Yet my soul is deaf to its call, heedless

So am I surprised
When I enter the sunset prayer
And my heart is inattentive, unaware?
Can the one who is blind, oblivious to Him all day,
See divine light and glory,
When he bows down to pray?

Dirty Dishes

        Piled high and greasy,
     Leaning stacks of dishes,
Dripping,
    Dribbling,
Splashing thick, dark gravy
   On the wall, counters, floor,
Everywhere

Just when I think,
There couldn't be more filth,
The sudsy, gravy pool in my sink
Overflows,

Sending the sprinting kids
      Sliding in gravy streaks
          And rivers of grease
               Across   the   kitchen   floor…

I feel my exasperation bubble,
Rise
like
hot steam
I glance at the tantrum toddler pummelling my knees,
And I want to scream

But… I don't
I close my eyes and breathe,
Grit my teeth to trap the scream
Very slowly, I unclench my fists,
Invoke Him, seek a gear change,
A paradigm shift

And then I open my eyes…
Surprise, surprise,
It's all the same
Dishes beckon, havoc reigns

And yet…
Whilst I feel burden's heavy pain,
The quality of my load's changed
I'm suddenly overwhelmed, strained,
By the weight of undeserved grace

In the overflowing dishes, river of gravy,
I perceive a surge of undue mercy
What's a dirty kitchen, flooding sink,
If not signs of ample provision,
Abundant blessing?

And perhaps I've been too preoccupied (or tired!) to consider,
That the weary, dedicated mother
Is truly a favourite of His court,

Crowned and jewelled
With the noblest role, loftiest pursuits

How quickly I've forgotten that I
Am the light of His compassionate eye,
Graced with a gift, beautiful beyond measure:
A heart so tender,
Selfless,
It reflects
Divine love

Teacher

I was a lonely, listless soul,
A fish out of water, a kite in a storm
Flailing and floundering, my cries
Whistled in the wind and died

Leaving only the silence of a barren home,
Bequeathed by working parents never home
No brothers, no sisters, no-one to care,
To listen, understand... just be there!

And so I ran, I ran far from the pain within,
Immersing myself in novels, music, utopian, love-filled imaginings
Yet I soon found, stories end, illusions fade,
An aimless life cannot be daydreamed away

What I knew, I refused to face,
I cared not to heal, only escape
So I turned to alcohol, cannabis, speed,
Anything to induce a numbing, dulling peace

I was drunk, I was stoned, yet my cup would not fill,
Shame and despair scoured me still
I was falling into a blackness so deep,
All hope in love's light ceased

I would have disappeared into that vector
Giving myself up to darkness forever
I had no purpose, no reason to live
I did not matter, I did not exist

Yet, just when I'd lost all will to cope
There filtered through, a faint ray of love, a bearer of hope
She penetrated the darkness, dispersed it ever so slightly
I could not believe it - did someone really care about my misery?

The dam that contained my frustration suddenly gave way,
Releasing a torrent of tears, bitterness, pain
My barriers down, I shouted, sobbed, ranted without fear
Having found, perhaps for the first time,
A true friend, an empathetic ear

Of all the people I had met, she alone cared to listen
Without judgement, anger, derision
When she looked at me, she saw beyond my black and heavy sins,
To their roots of suffering within

This sixty year old granny, a stranger until that day
Saw I was a mess, but did not wrinkle her nose and turn away,
Nor did she offer platitudes, warnings, unsolicited advice

Her open mind and heart healed me more than any words might
I did not find life's purpose and my soul's strength, overnight
I struggled for a very long time
But ultimately, it was the love of my teacher that saw me through
Before its light, the shadows of cynicism and despair, withdrew,

Enabling me to see beauty and love where once I could not,
Opening my heart to divine purpose when once it was lost
As soon as I could see and feel compassion,
It was only a matter of time,
Before I saw its source in compassion divine

I have had many teachers, who have taught me many things
But there was only one who taught me how to truly live
She loved God and exuded this love with all her being
It was through her, that I discovered the sweetness of Love
And for Love, living.

Mother

I was immersed in dark waters deep,
Unable to see, breathe, or speak,
Tiny, vulnerable, utterly weak

Like breath to life, sun to seed,
You sustained my every need
From you I emerged, a human being

A feisty, bawling, bundle of burden,
Screaming without the slightest compunction,
Demanding constant care, perpetual attention

Exhausting days stretched into many a year,
A seamless continuum of struggle and prayer,
Revealing unparalleled devotion and care

How many sacrifices you made!
Difficulties and challenges you overcame,
Tantrums and trials you forgave,
To nurture my character, my soul, my faith!

Tears choke me, my debt I fail to express
Yet one thing, I cannot leave unsaid,
Lest it is buried with my dying breath

Above all, dearest mother,
You showed me, like no other
A love akin to the love of my Maker

You were, you are, a beautiful mirror
Reflecting the light of my Creator
Your abiding care, selflessness,
Alludes to the Source of grace itself

In an unjust, callous world, wracked by pain,
Where greed abounds and darkness reigns,
I might never have seen divine light prevail,

Had I not, from the moment I arrived,
Seen in your compassion and sacrifice,
Night dispersed by glowing moonlight

For amidst the darkness and shadows cruel
Who reflects the Sun's beauty, love, truth,
Better than the splendorous moon?

My Shadow

Night and day, rain or shine,
My shadow follows close behind

Soft brown eyes, pensive,
Quick to grasp, attentive,
Her innocent, watchful gaze
Absorbing every gesture and phrase

She echoes my laughter and sighs,
Mimics my expressions and cries,
Assimilates without critique,
My values, attitude, beliefs
Merrily, she traipses behind me,
Mirroring whatever she sees

As I interact, so does she
As I chide her, she chides me
I am her aspiration, model of perfection
She wants to grow up to be just like me

But I worry, how long will she be
So small, looking up at me?
How long will her pure heart and soul
Perceive all flaws
As colourful shades of a beautiful rainbow?

When her mind grows judicious, wise,
To see as clearly as her eyes,
Will her heart sink with dismay,
To find contradictions, pretence and role-play?

Where she saw faith, prayer, devotion,
Will she find distraction, empty motion?
Where she saw vigour and candour,
Will she find suppressed bitterness, anger?

Will the charm and sweetness she adored,
Be exposed as flattery, fraud?
Will my passion for truth and justice
Ring hollow ... preaching without practice?

When my child truly sees
The truth with all its subtleties,
Will she still raise her beautiful eyes
To the skies and plead,
'I want to be just like my Mummy, please?'

Empathy

Although I have not experienced
The gnawing loneliness,
Deep yearning or anger,
Masked by her steely exterior,

I perceive,
And feel,
Something of her anguish
Tear me up within,

And constrained by her pain,
My heart aches,

As I discern
How isolation hurts,
Anger burns,
Guilt torments,
Worry upends...

So unsolicited,
I reach out,

With subtlety,
Understanding and care,
Almost like I've been there,

And though I'm aware,
I cannot wand-wave,
And wish it all away,

I can
Listen keenly,
Feel deeply,
Offer care and support
Sensitively,
Sincerely

I have come to realise
That when someone cares enough
To truly empathise,

The solace and strength she brings,
May be just what is needed to begin
Healing.

A Mother in Palestine

At every moment, you fight
With every choking breath, you strive
With every fiery tear, you inspire
...Do I?

Youthful sons incarcerated,
Ageing husband assassinated,
Feeble mother shelled in her bed,
Brutal casualties of Cast Lead
A sleeping angel survives, tossing in terror,
Nightly haunted by blood and snipers and massacre,

At every moment, you fight
With every choking breath, you strive
With every fiery tear, you inspire
...Do I?

For your child, a brave smile creasing your worn face
Father is with Grandma, in God's embrace
Your brothers will return, have faith in God's grace
Loneliness will fade, fear abates, have faith, have faith!

At every moment, you fight
With every choking breath, you strive
With every fiery tear, you inspire
... Do I?

You face the glass gaze with unwavering eyes
As he sneers, spits, barks and pries
Hour upon hour of callous indignity,
Checkpoint upon checkpoint, day after day, to teach, to survive,
Borne with raised chin and flashing eyes,
Silent resilience, unbroken dignity, undying fire,
Infusing your tired, bent frame behind the barbed wire

You return to a crumbling concrete confine,
Walls scarred by bullets and shell-fire,
Wracked by agonising, lonely silence,
Echoes of laughter long subsided

At every moment, you fight
With every choking breath, you strive
With every fiery tear, you inspire
...*Do I?*

I claim, I profess, I believe,
In your call for justice, freedom, peace
Your supporter, friend, sister,
...*Am I?*

I know, I weep, I pray,
I rise, I struggle, I fight for you everyday
...*Do I?*

Silent Plea

Deep within me,
In the pit of my belly,
A nauseating, convulsive fear
Consumes me

When I wake, when I sleep,
All moments in between,
Permeate a damp, palpable
Dread

Sometimes, I distract myself with fantasies,
Illusive possibilities -
Belonging, security,
Love, home,
Even family...

I'm so lost in hope's reverie,
I can almost ignore the sickly churning within me,
Auguring a battery
Of curses, punches,
Rib-cracking kicks,
My uncle's steely eyes,
Curled lip, ringed fists...

School is my solace,
My escape from a cage,
Rank with fear, mottled by pain

Until the bell rings
And my heart sinks
I wave at my teacher,
My smile thin, wan,
Silently pleading with her,
A friend, parent, anyone!

Please!
See the tremor in my step,
The faint swelling of my face,
The terror behind my blank gaze,

And save me!

Before my worn spirit drowns
In fear's cavernous,
Choking,
Abyss

Liberty

Covered with care,
Every contour and hair,
She is modesty, poise, intellect,
Love for God manifest

A lone burning flame
Lit by the oil of resilient faith,
Undiminished by blank stares,
Crude slurs, scathing glares

Undimmed by prejudice and isolation,
Job exclusion, social discrimination
All the pain of French disdain
Masquerading as liberty and laicité

She is French by nationality,
French by birth and residency,
Citizen of a secular democracy,
Yet stripped of her basic rights and liberties

Rights to state education,
Job equality, career progression,
Right to integrate *without* assimilation,

All because she desires
Value and dignity defined
By the quality of her character and mind,
Rather than cosmetics, curves and hemlines

Across the Channel, through the fog,
Penetrating even the London drear and smog,
Her enduring glow unsettles me,
Sparking self-doubt, perplexity

Legally, I am free
To practice my faith publicly
I'm cosseted by a culture of tolerance,
Diversity, liberty, even acceptance

And yet, I choose wilfully to conform,
Bare and beautify by the norm,
Undercutting my faith and my identity,
For fashion, career, delusions of social credibility

I always believed she was bound and I was free
Yet if true liberty is strength, tenacity,
Courage to actualise principles and identity,

Then who is chained, trapped, weak...
And who is strong and free?

Born to Dream

I gaze above, afar,
Searching for my North Star
Seeking beyond desire's reach,
I was born to dream

Gawking at the gutters and greed around me
Binds me to the grim and grimy
Raising my sights to divinity, beauty, flight,
Sets my true aspirations alight

I work, I eat, I sleep
I function on a daily routine
Yet in heart and mind, I can transcend,
Traverse a higher realm

A realm of purpose, discovery,
Of who I am and who I choose to be
Where love, grace, purity,
Surpass abstract theory,
To be the essence of my being

Society, of course, is not conducive to dreaming
Idealising is idling
Time is money, money success
Spirituality, selflessness,

Rarely accrue in pounds and pence

And yet, don't social revolutions, world peace,
Depend on dreamers with lofty ideals?
The vision, courage, tenacity,
To see a better world and make it a reality?

Without idealists, dreamers,
Who would be the Mandelas, Mother Theresas?
Who would fight American hegemony,
Israeli apartheid, Saudi bigotry,
Or even the vice within oneself or community?

Who would champion the plight
Of those stripped of their basic rights?
Would anyone really care
To save the victims of poverty, ignorance, despair?

I return to myself; I ask candidly,
Dreamer, scrooge, cynic - who will I be?
Will I look beyond self-interest
To realise a more compassionate self,

Or will I eventually die,
With shrivelled heart and cold eyes,
Complicit in perpetuating
The pain of the wretched and deprived?

Compassion

Sometimes,
I breathe in
The spicy, creamy aroma
Of my favourite, steaming pasta,

And I'm about to dig in,
When an image passes through my mind,
The distended belly, gaunt face,
Hungry eyes,
Of a starving child

Sometimes,
I'm snug under the covers,
Burrowed in a favourite book and sweater,
Oblivious to sleet and thunder,

When I suddenly consider
Children blue and huddled together,
Each ragged breath, frozen tear,
A piercing dagger
In the heart of their mother

Sometimes,
I'm chatting away,
Enjoying coffee and creme brûlée
With friends in a café,

When it occurs to me,
That for so many,
Clean water on a scorching day
Requires a back-breaking, five-mile journey

In the moments that I venture
Outside my middle-class bubble,
I'm wracked with guilt,
I feel ashamed, sick
How self-absorbed, selfish
I am!

For many of us
Who live in comfort,
Fleeting twinges of conscience
Are common

Yet,
Does the spark of compassion
Ever sustain a revolution
Beyond sporadic donations?

Rare is the one who truly cares
To recalibrate
The compass of his life,
Enough to forswear
Luxury and laissez-faire,
For reflective, equitable, ethical
Living

A Plastic Life

'With more than eight million tonnes going into the oceans every year, it is estimated there will be more plastic than fish by 2050 and 99 per cent of all the seabirds on the planet will have consumed some. It is thought the sea now contains some 51 trillion microplastic particles – 500 times more than stars in our galaxy.'

(The Independent, 28 September 2017)

As a
Gurgling, burbling, growing baby,
I constantly fed
On a plastic bottle
And slept with a plastic dummy
In my plastic cot

I nibbled on plastic rings,
Crawled in plastic diapers
And drooled on plastic toys,
Before I was weaned
In plastic bowls,
Aided by plastic spoons,
In a plastic, easy to clean, chair

I soon outgrew my plastic lego and dolls,
To kick around plastic footballs,
And slouch on the couch,

Glued to the glossy TV, PS4 and Xbox,
When I wasn't studying and surfing on my plastic laptop

Successful admission into university
Led to a life of never-ending study,
Powered by plastic-sealed, ready meals
And countless, bottled energy drinks

The years flew by and before I knew it,
I'd graduated to a high-flying career
Of smart plastic suits and posh plastic shoes,
Affording endless plastic bags of designer shopping,
A whole new level of synthetic, luxury living

And now, I've finally retired
I've shifted from city to seaside,
To relax in plastic shades and shorts,
Hydrate on bottled water
And enjoy plastic water sports

And I guess in old age,
I'll survive on plastic-packaged pills
And shuffle around with a plastic stick,
Before I remove my plastic teeth,
And plastic bifocals
To drift off
To eternal sleep.

Façades

Everything,

It seems,
Is either wrapped in reams

Of glossy paper,
Or sealed in flashy containers,

Or packaged
In sleek bags

Or validated
By branded labels

I've sometimes wondered
How far the lines are blurred

Between false trimmings
And true spirit

Am I not easily sold
On fool's gold,

Duped by glamour and style,
Image and guile?

In fact,
How far have I lost my way

In the mirror maze
Of a synthetic age?

Irony

Before the mirror every morn,
I scrutinise my face and adorn
With varying sheen, shade, and tints,
My eyes, skin and lips

Then I carefully accessorise
My artful attire,
So all's in perfect sync
With catwalk 'in'

Yet,
Now and again,
I'm plagued
By questions disconcerting,
A weariness creeping in...

How much of my energy is drained
By the struggle to maintain
A pretty figure and face?

How many detoxing, anti-ageing products will I buy
In my compulsive desire to defy
The greying of age, wrinkling of time?

Is it not futile
To resist my body's natural decline
And mortality's relentless rise?

So then why
Am I obsessed with my outside?

Is it because deep down, I fear
That if my youth and beauty disappear
And I am left
Old, feeble, and bent,
I will lose the key
To success, acceptance, felicity?

And is that fear made deeper still,
By the sickening awareness within,
That I've been so preoccupied
With transient desire,

I've actually ignored
My soul's true north,
Seeking lasting peace
In the fleeting breeze?

And now, when youth's veneer
And strength begin to disappear,
I realise -
What immaturity, vacuity, it hides!

So perhaps,
I should throw paint and powder to the wind,
Abandon façades and focus within

Before death comes silently knocking,
Let me, in earnest, begin fostering
Beauty of soul and being,
Deep,
Real,
Lasting.

How Conscious am I?

How conscious am I
Of the days and hours fleeting by?

Do I see how spring's brazen flush is soon cowed
By winter's cold and dark shroud?
And bright, frolicking days
Always give way
To night's ever-looming shade?

Am I aware that round my ears, my hair's slightly greyed?
And I can no longer bound up and down the stairs
Or survive on 2 hours' sleep in the same old way?

How long will I slumber?
Will I stir
Or will I wait
For death to jar me awake?

Runaway Train

'Surprise!' 'Happy 40th', scream the silver banner,
Garish balloons and streamers
'40's the new 30!'
Live it up, sky dive, splurge on a dream holiday!

And I do...
I do it all,
Spa days, hiking, biking, makeovers galore,
Even a child-free, second honeymoon,
Basking in the romance of faded youth

So why do I find myself, of late,
At night, lying awake,
Uneasy, queasy... afraid?

Like a lone, half-blind driver
At the helm of a racing train,
Hurtling forward at dizzying speed,
Unsure where it will lead

It's exhilarating, bracing, fun,
A whirlwind of perpetual motion!
Yet unnerving, disorienting, insipid,
A sensory blur, no meaning or spirit

So I slam down the brakes,
And life chugs along at a far duller pace,
Work, kids, work, sleep,
A mechanical, clockwork routine...

Fast or slow, right or left,
What does it really matter?
I have no ultimate end in mind
If life's a journey, I'm only in it for the ride

And yet,

I am loathed to lead a runaway train,
Veering and careening towards a blind fate
Through dark, desolate nights,
I grope for truth, direction,
Light

For so long, I have lived
In worldly shadow and spectre,
Oblivious to beauty and truth immaterial
...Is it too late to start over?

I raise filled eyes,
Trembling hands
'My Lord, I am 40...
My youth squandered, passed,
Yet let maturity be a journey to You,
To Beauty, Love and Peace unsurpassed.'

To What End

When I move on
To the realm beyond,

Contrary to what people say,
I will not regret the day

I did not seize the chance
To enjoy life's heady dance

Nor will I be filled with remorse
Because I didn't relax more

Or kick myself
For not working less

I doubt I'll care
How much I've saved that year

Or how much I've spent
On pampering myself
In fact, when I hear the clichés,
'Forget tomorrow, live for today,'

'The future's uncertain,
Always begin with dessert,'

I wonder if I'm not being misled…
Would I not be better off instead

If I lived not for the moment,
But for the eternity that comes next?

Time

I rat-race against time,
A mindless, mechanised blur,
Acquisition-driven, checklist-led,
My spirit numbing, succumbing, lifeless

How do I fight the inexorable passing of Time?
Resist routine's relentless grind?
By forever doing more,
Feeling less?
By swapping depth and stillness
For utility, efficiency, pace?

Or, is it the other way round?
Do I need to slow down,
End the obsessive race
For maximum material gain
And strive for a plane beyond,
Where time ceases, dissolves?

Have I ever glimpsed the beauty of transcending time
Through secret communion with the Sublime,
In the silence of reflection,
Clarity of introspection,
In abandoning my ego and desire
To serve the Divine?

Have I felt the truth of timelessness
In compassion and selflessness,
In seeing beauty within the ordinary,
Finding purpose in adversity,
In weeping to Him through dark nights,
Overwhelmed by love and humility?

Have I realised that mortality and transience
Can only be surpassed by true existence,
When I actualise my potential, my immensity,
And my soul breathes
Beauty, humanity, peace

Whirlwind

Caught
In a vortex of incessant activity,
Material dust and debris,
I am a racing, chasing, blur
Plunging
In obscurity

Dimly,
I struggle,
Through a manic, scheduled mist
An anxious whirlwind,
Spinning
In soulless vacuity

Am I driven to distraction
Or does the tempest lie
In my own restless, fickle mind,
Charging in dogged pursuit
Of a million, material lies?

If only,
I can will,
My turbulent self,
Be still…

In stillness,
The dust settles,
Storm clears,
Darkness lifts

In stillness
And silence,
I can begin
To see
And seek
Wholeness, purpose,
Peace.

Maybe Later

Indulgence
Led by appetite,
Chasing carnal delight,
Revelling, bingeing, doping,
Anything to keep the cheap thrills going
...Too busy having fun, maybe later...

Love
Fallen and fallen hard,
Enamoured by endearment and charm
Dreaming, pining, flying on nine,
Giddy with desire, blood on fire
...Too impassioned to think, maybe later...

Ambition
Driven by insatiable hunger
For money, luxury, power
Descending at destructive speed
In a senseless spiral of greed
...Too obsessed to bother, maybe later...

Retirement
Feet up, need to relax, rest
Done with work, struggle, doing my best
Had my kids, made my money, tasted success

Time to finally enjoy, unwind, retire in Dorset
...By the beach, snoozing... maybe later

Death
Soul in my throat, sick with regret…
All the good I could have done!
All that I could have become!
No strength, no breath
...No time, too late.

Vision

I can be
All that I can see,
What I cannot see
I cannot aspire to be

So maybe,
I should be
Still

And think deeply,
See keenly,
Envision clearly,
What it is I truly
Long to be

If I don't,
I'll be wont
To chase rainbows,
All that glitters
And glimmers
But is ephemeral

So first,
I must emerge

From confusion,
Illusion,
All that muddies my capacity
To see my highest, potential reality

Once I truly see
All my latent perfection and beauty,
I can spread my wings
And finally begin
To fly

Freedom

Through the laughter,
Hubbub and chatter,
Despite expectations,
Attitudes and relations,

I am free

Whatever the social variables,
Norms and determiners,
No matter the pressures,

I am free

Whatever my circle,
However controlled or liberal,
Whatever the power dynamics,
Currents and struggles,

I am free

Whatever my situation,
Status and position,
No matter my limitations,
Fears and frustrations,

I am free

I do not deny
So many factors
Are beyond my power,
Affecting and influencing
Who I am, how I think

Yet ultimately,

My conscience is mine alone
My soul and will are my own

Whether I succumb to vice,
Or far above it, I rise,

Whether I clip the wings of my soul,
Or lift them to soar,

Whether I fall,

Or fly,

The choice is mine

www.ingramcontent.com/pod-product-compliance
Lightning Source LLC
Chambersburg PA
CBHW071317080526
44587CB00018B/3263